G-O-D Spells Good

The Christian Science Publishing Society
Boston, Massachusetts, U.S.A.

Other publications of interest

Bible Stories for Children*
Colonel Mustard and the Hay Customers
They Decided to Pray
Too many angels to count
What Prayer Does

Audiocassettes
Before we read
Being a family
Follow and Rejoice

*book and audiocassette

This article by Marquita Shiells Griswold appeared in the
Christian Science Sentinel, December 7, 1992
Article adapted for publication in booklet format.
Booklet design and illustration: Christina J. Cannard

Printed in the United States of America.

THIS BOOK BELONGS TO

____

(please write your name here)

This book tells the true story of Ann and a Sunday School lesson that helped her one day when she wasn't feeling well. Ann remembered learning that God is good and cares for all of His children all the time—she knew that God included her in that care and then she was fine.

Ann attends the Christian Science Sunday School where she learns many important lessons about God from the Bible and *Science and Health with Key to the Scriptures* by Mary Baker Eddy.

The tire swing hanging from a huge tree in the backyard was Ann's favorite thing to play on. Ann was four now.

One afternoon Mom asked Ann's big brother Glen to look after Ann and their brother Paul while she took their sister Janet to a flute lesson. The three kids went out to play in the backyard.

The flute lesson was almost over when the teacher's telephone rang.

It was Glen. “Mom, something is wrong with Ann. She says she doesn’t feel well. Please come home right away.”

Mom assured Glen she'd be right home. "Don't be afraid, Glen. Your Father-Mother God is already right there with you. God is taking care of Ann. Remember 'All, all is well,' as the hymn we sing in Sunday School tells us."

Mom and Janet arrived home quickly. Glen was relieved. Mom sent Glen and Janet into the backyard with Paul. She wanted to be alone with Ann so the two of them could pray together. It had always helped the family to turn to God in prayer whenever there was trouble.

Ann was on the sofa. Mom put her arms around Ann and gave her a big hug. Then she sat down next to her.

Ann said, "Mommy, I don't feel good. My tummy really hurts."

Mom was praying silently to God. "I know there is the right thing to say to Ann that will help her," she thought. Very soon she had an idea. She remembered that Ann was just learning the letters of the alphabet and could spell a few words. Ann knew how to spell *God.* Now Mom knew the right thing to say.

"Ann, how do you spell *God?"*

"G–O–D."

"That's right. Very good! Now what have you learned about God in Sunday School?"

"God is Love."

"Yes. God is Love. God loves and cares for each one of us. We're certainly glad about that, aren't we? What else can you tell me about God?"

Ann thought for a moment. "Well, God is everywhere, all around us." And she stretched out her arms in a wide circular motion to show she knew God was all around and everywhere.

"That's true," agreed Mom. "Did you know that God is also *good?*"

Ann nodded. "We learned that in Sunday School, too."

"I'm so glad you already know that. The very first book in the Bible teaches us that God makes everything and that everything He makes is good. And Christ Jesus proved that's true by healing people. So, if God is good and is everywhere, and God makes everything good, there can only be *good.* Isn't that right?"

"I guess so," nodded Ann.

"Then that means that there can't really be anything bad. In all of God's universe, everywhere, there is only good. That's the truth. Because that's the truth, then everything about *you,* as God's perfect child, His reflection, is good, too. There can't be anything to make you feel bad. God makes you good and keeps you good."

Mom could tell Ann was thinking about this. Then Mom said,

"Ann, how do you suppose you spell the word *good?*"

"I don't know."

"Well, it's easy." Mom explained, "You know how to spell *God.* G–O–D. *Good* is spelled exactly like *God,* except there are two *O*'s in the middle instead of just one. G–O–O–D, good."

"G–O–O–D, good. I can spell *good!* G–O–O–D!" Suddenly Ann brightened up. She sat up. She smiled a big smile. "God is good and I'm all good. Oh, thank you, Mommy.

My tummy doesn't hurt anymore. I'm all right. I want to go out and play." With that, she jumped down off the sofa and ran into the backyard.

Glen saw Ann running. He was surprised. "Mom, what happened?"

Mom smiled. "Well, what do you think happened? Your little sister just had a healing; that's what happened. When Ann understood that God is good and that everything He made is good, including her, she was healed. It was as simple as that. I'm so glad that what is true for Ann is true for all of God's children." Glen agreed.

The four kids slid on the slide, swung on the tire swing, played games, and turned somersaults on the grass until suppertime. And Mom thanked God for answering her prayer to know the right thing to say to Ann.

Afterword

Christian Science was discovered by Mary Baker Eddy, whose book *Science and Health with Key to the Scriptures* explains the laws of God, good, by which Christ Jesus healed. You can find *Science and Health* in bookstores or Christian Science Reading Rooms.

Your telephone book will have the address of Christian Science Churches, which have Sunday Schools where you and your friends are always welcome.

NP9604020